<u>INDEX</u>

Imad Mughniyeh

Imad Mughniyeh was born in 1962 in the Lebanese Shi'ite village of Tayr Dibba to a poor family of olive and lemon harvesters. He moved to Beirut as a child and despite his religious affiliation, he became active in the predominantly Sunni Palestinian al-Fatah movement.

In Lebanese Palestinian reports, Mughniyeh was even described as participating in the unit of bodyguards protecting then-PLO chief Yasser Arafat. But after the PLO chairman and his fighters were forced to leave Lebanon following the Israeli invasion in 1982 – just three years after the Islamic Revolution in Iran – Mughniyeh returned to his own religious cohort and joined Hezbollah, "The Party of God," a heavily armed Lebanese faction established and nurtured by Iran.

He quickly involved himself in some of the most outrageous Hezbollah attacks, proving his loyalty and his skills. He was trained by the chillingly skilled Iranian Revolutionary Guard Corps.

In a bloody two-year period – between November 1982 and September 1984 – he was a key player in several car bombing attacks against Israeli, American, and French targets in Lebanon. Among his trademarks: videotapes made by the suicide bombers and their accomplices nearby. The terrifying impact was thus magnified.

The attacks of those years included two assaults on Israeli military headquarters in the southern city of Tyre, which killed 150 Israelis and Lebanese.

He orchestrated the suicide bombings of the U.S. Marines barracks and a French military building in Beirut, killing 241 American servicemen, 58 French paratroopers, and six Lebanese civilians.

He was also a major actor in the bombing of the 1984 U.S. Embassy in Beirut, which killed 63 people. And this was just the beginning. His career would mushroom over the next two and a half decades.

In 1985, Mughniyeh personally participated in the hijacking of a TWA airliner. After it was forced to land in Beirut, a U.S. Navy diver among the passengers – Robert Stethem – was tortured and killed.

The first image of Mughniyeh, then just 22 years old, was first seen in the pages of the Western press when photographed waving his pistol near the TWA pilot's head in the cockpit. That photo was the key evidence used by U.S. law enforcement officials to indict Mughniyeh for murder in that incident. But for Israel, it would take another seven years to realize his significance.

The Hezbollah man was the architect of the 1992 bombing of the Israeli Embassy in Buenos Aires, Argentina, which killed 29 people – including seven Israelis, among them one Mossad agent. This was Mughniyeh's revenge for the Israeli helicopter attack that had killed Hezbollah's top leader, Abbas Moussawi.

The Buenos Aires attack led Israel to acknowledge two important facts: One, that Mughniyeh would avenge every Israeli attack on his organization; and two, that Mughniyeh had to be wiped out.

These realizations were further strengthened by an attack two years later, when along with his Iranian patrons, Mughniyeh masterminded the bombing of the Jewish community center in the Argentinian capital, which devastated the building and left 85 people dead.

From that point on, Israel used every opportunity it could to try to get rid of Mughniyeh. Numerous tentative plans were drawn up, but only three came into fruition.

In 1994, the Mossad conspired a devious plan to obliterate Mughniyeh: Lebanese agents working for the Mossad planted a car bomb aimed at Mughniyeh's brother Fuad. Anticipating that Mughniyeh would attend his brother's funeral, Israel planned to carry out their assassination of the Hezbollah military chief then: But Imad Mughniyeh, probably paranoid about possible attempts on his life, did not show up at the funeral.

A few months after Fuad's death, Israeli intelligence managed to obtain precise information that Imad Mughniyeh was scheduled to board a flight from Damascus to Tehran using a false name.

The Mossad informed the CIA of Mughniyeh's whereabouts, and the Americans orchestrated a redirection of the flight to Kuwait and dispatched a military plane from Saudi Arabia to bring Mughniyeh to justice in the U.S. courts.

But the CIA made a cardinal error: It disclosed to the Kuwaitis the identity of the wanted terrorist. Fearing retribution from Hezbollah should they accede to the U.S. demand, the Kuwaitis declined to order the passengers of the plane to disembark. Kuwait permitted the flight to take off to Tehran.

The next missed opportunity was completely the Israelis' fault. After the Israeli withdrawal from Lebanon in 2000, the senior echelon of Hezbollah – known as the top five – paraded along the Israeli border on a victorious patrol tour. Mughniyeh was among them.

Israeli reconnaissance photographed the five and transmitted the images to Aman (military intelligence) headquarters in Tel Aviv. They were identified; and an attack plan was put into motion. Drone aircraft that could fire missiles were launched.

Western intelligence sources say they were told by Israelis later that this was a "rare opportunity to disrupt Hezbollah's leadership." But the order to kill never came. Prime Minister Ehud Barak, who was proud of ordering the Israeli withdrawal from south Lebanon after 18 years of occupation, feared that the relative calm would be disrupted if he had Hebzollah's top leaders eliminated.

Senior officers in the Mossad were furious. Years of painstaking information-gathering efforts were wasted. But they had no choice but to accept their political leader's decision and to wait for the next opportunity.

Mughniyeh, as the years went by, became more cautious. Israeli intelligence learned that he went to a plastic surgeon in Beirut to alter his appearance.

He also moved to the safe haven of Tehran, where he enhanced his professional and personal ties with the Revolutionary Guards commanders – particularly with the charismatic General Qassem Soleimani, who was head of the elite Al-Quds force.

After returning to his Beirut headquarters, Mughniyeh continued to travel frequently among the triangle of the capitals of Lebanon, Syria and Iran.

The Mossad hunters, experts in human weaknesses and knowing that nobody is immune to error, waited patiently – but desperately.

Mughniyeh did indeed make mistakes, basically feeling too safe in the Syrian capital. He went to Damascus for both business and pleasure.

For his bloody business, he would meet with his master and friend, Iranian General Soleimani, to coordinate and plot strategy. Often joining them was General Muhammad Suleiman, top security adviser to Syrian President Bashar Assad and the man in charge of the regime's nuclear reactor and its special military ties with Iran and Hezbollah.

After working hours, Mughniyeh would enjoy the pleasures that Damascus had to offer: good food, alcohol and women – most of which he would not risk indulging in back home in the religious Shi'ite neighborhoods of Beirut.

Details of the "operation"

Piecing together human intelligence and telephone intercepts, Israeli intelligence managed to learn a great deal about Mughniyeh's private life and tracked his movements, finally aware of his post-plastic surgery appearance. They took advantage of two human weaknesses, quite uncharacteristic for a master terrorist on the run.

First, hosted by Syrian intelligence in one of its guest apartments, and in constant contact with Iranian "diplomats," Mughniyeh felt totally comfortable in Damascus. Living for decades with the assumption that he was an assassination target, he must have craved a place to feel safe. He let down his guard when in Syria, moving around with full self-confidence and no fear.

He also permitted himself to do, in Damascus, what he did not do at home in Lebanon: fool around with women. That, too, meant that he was literally a man about town, in moving cars more than a cautious man would be. Spies for the Mossad took note of routes that he repeatedly took.

Mughniyeh had an apartment in the posh neighborhood of Kafr Sousa, home to Syria's most wealthy businessmen and the military and intelligence cronies of the Assad regime. Feeling safe and secure due to his altered appearance and years of evading assassination attempts, Mughniyeh would travel in his **SUV** from Beirut to Damascus without bodyguards, often with his personal driver but sometimes alone.

Mughniyeh and other Hizbullah men lowered their guard and were relaxed while in Damascus, believing that they were beyond Israel's reach. Mughniyeh was walking alone, when a car bomb exploded.

The Mossad recruited a Syrian expat who visited his country often, and asked him to move to Damascus to provide logistics for the operation. The agent provided a villa to hide the vehicle and affix it with explosives, in addition to accommodations for the group that carried out the operation.

He rented the villa in an upscale suburb of Damascus ("Assad Villages"), located to the northwest of Kfar Sousa, and asked an ironsmith to separate the car entrance from the pedestrian entrance with an iron net on three sides, making it look like a cage and blocking the entry to the villa from that location.

A while later, the agent went back to Syria and bought a Mitsubishi Pajero 4×4, after knowing that several similar makes visited the targeted location often. In addition, Mughniyeh sometimes drove the same make. The execution team used a different model, Mitsubishi Lancer, due to its popularity in Syria in general.

The Pajero, now parked in the villa, was equipped with explosives in its trunk door. It was later discovered that, in addition to the explosives, the bomb contained metal pellets that can cause extensive damage to the target instantaneously. The device was similar to several bombs used by Israel to assassinate leaders in Lebanon and abroad.

The investigators and people close to the file are very secretive about the implementation team. But there are indicators that show that they were not Syrian citizens and that they had travelled in and out of the country to implement the operation.

In the early afternoon of 12 February 2008, one of the implementers drove the Pajero, equipped with explosives in its trunk door, and parked it outside the building frequented by Mughniyeh.

At dusk, the team of four individuals took the getaway Lancer and, after making sure that the construction workers had left the building under **construction** next to Mughniyeh's building, three of them went upstairs to observe the parking lot, the target, and the vehicle with the explosives.

They chose an apartment on the sixth floor. One of them surveyed the area with binoculars, another was charged with detonating the explosives, and the third was for protection. The fourth waited in the getaway car parked at the back of the building close to the fence.

Right before 10:20 pm, Mughniyeh exited the building and, as soon as he reached the well-lit lot nine meters away from the Pajero, the bomb was detonated and he was killed instantly.

Pe'al!" ordered the senior Mossad commander in charge of this extraordinary mission. Translated from Hebrew, this meant Go. Act. Push the button. The expert sitting beside the commander obeyed the order. He pushed the button. One hundred and thirty-five miles (215 km.) away in Syria's capital, Damascus, an explosion tore a notorious terrorist to bits.

The explosion was heard around 10:20 pm. Some people rushed to the location, including those Mughniyeh was seeing in the apartment. It turned out that when Mughniyeh had stepped out of the building's main gate, a 2006 silver Mitsubishi Pajero 4×4 parked nine meters away exploded, killing him alone, on the spot.

The implementing team left the building and headed toward their getaway car. They immediately drove toward the Mazzeh highway where they parked the car on the side of the road and left behind some items for distraction. The investigations showed that the implementing team faced a problem while escaping, which led them to leave the car and use another to escape to an unknown location.

This was a triumph for the men and women of Israeli intelligence. They had accomplished the nearly impossible. Their feeling was similar to the satisfaction Americans would enjoy, three years later, when Navy Seals found and killed Osama bin Laden.

A manhunt lasting a quarter of a century had come to an end. At Mossad headquarters at the Glilot Junction north of Tel Aviv there was great relief and even celebration.

In a most unusual example of operational cooperation, a CIA liaison officer was also in the Mossad HQ – part of the logistics and decision-making process for the assassination. The Israelis understood that officials at CIA headquarters in Langley, Virginia, were also very pleased.

Yet Israelis close to their country's intelligence agencies are telling Western officials something different: that the operation was almost entirely "blue and white" – referring to the colors of Israel's flag – with hardly any "red, white, and blue."

The Israelis were surprised to learn, during strategic talks with their counterparts in Washington, that the Americans were just as eager to get rid of him.

Since 1975, the CIA had been forbidden by Congress to carry out assassinations – even of America's worst enemies. But that policy changed after 9/11, when President George W. Bush ordered targeted killings using drone aircraft.

Nevertheless, in the eyes of the Bush administration – though not always understood by the Israelis – there was a huge difference between sending assassins and killing targets from the sky.

At a certain point during consultations with the Americans, then-Mossad director Meir Dagan proposed to his CIA counterpart, Gen. Michael Hayden, a joint operation to eliminate Mughniyeh.

Gen. Michael Hayden (as CIA director under President George W. Bush) agreed, but he set two conditions: First, that no innocent people would be hurt: The Americans were very concerned by the proximity of Mughniyeh's apartment to a girls' school; second, that only Mughniyeh would be targeted – and that none of his Syrian or Iranian acquaintances could be touched. The United States was reluctant to stir up violent conflicts with sovereign states.

At least according to what Israelis have been telling Western officials, the Mossad did not need the CIA for active management of the operation. They had already gleaned all the details necessary about Mughniyeh's daily routine and his hideout in Damascus.

The CIA was there, as they put it, to fill in any missing intelligence information and provide extra eyes in Damascus.

The Mossad certainly had its own excellent expertise, in its Kidon (Bayonet) special operations unit, when it came to killing terrorists. Still, the Israelis felt more comfortable having the CIA take part – even if the American role was seen as minor.

As agreed by Dagan and Hayden, a senior CIA official from its operations directorate was assigned to the Mossad team working on the project. The command center was in Tel Aviv.

Kidon operatives, along with Aman signals intelligence Unit 8200, monitored Mughniyeh almost around the clock, zooming in on his safe-house and the parking lot nearby. Based on previous operations, it can be assumed that the team had some physical presence in the area. It was decided that the weapon of choice would be a bomb planted in or on a car parked near Mughniyeh's apartment.

The CIA-Mossad relations hit a bump, for a while, when the Americans got cold feet and pulled out of the operation. The CIA began to reiterate its fears of the collateral damage that such an assassination would cause – concerned, despite Israel's assurances, about the girls' school nearby.

The Mossad was sorry to see the CIA pull out, but the preparations continued. Nevertheless, then-Prime Minister Ehud Olmert ordered the Mossad to make sure that the "killing zone" of the bomb be very narrow, so that only Mughniyeh would be touched.

The "toy factory" of the Mossad and the Aman agency – their technological units – began designing, assembling and testing the bomb. It was a laborious procedure, requiring dozens of tests, until the results were satisfactory and matched the guidelines stipulated by Olmert. The process was filmed, time and again, for analysis and dissection.

Contrary to the recent reports in the American media, the process of developing the bomb was carried out in Israel. Not in the U.S. Once Olmert was confident that the bomb would be highly accurate, officials say they have learned from Israel that Olmert brought the video clips to Washington. He showed them to President Bush and asked him to bring the CIA back into the operation. The video clearly showed that the diameter of the "killing zone" was no more than 10 meters. Bush was impressed. The next day, while he was still in the U.S., Olmert received a call from Dagan informing him that the CIA was back in.

The bomb was smuggled to Syria via Jordan, whose intelligence ties with the CIA and the Mossad had been tight and intimate for decades. The involvement of the CIA gave the Jordanians a sense of security in cooperating, in case of Hezbollah retribution.

There were two main obstacles to executing the operation. Mughniyeh's visits to his Damascus apartment were random and could not be predetermined by the surveillance teams. Secondly, it was difficult for the teams to ensure that they would be able to secure a spot for their rigged car to be parked near Mughniyeh or his vehicle.

Eventually, the conspirators found an undisclosed operational solution which would give them enough warning time ahead of Mughniyeh's arrival to prepare the trap.

The day of the assassination arrived: On the evening of February 12, Mughniyeh's car was spotted pulling into the parking lot. The Mossad planners breathed a sigh of relief. The school nearby was closed for the night. Even if the bomb was unexpectedly flawed, the innocent school girls were not at risk.

But to the agony of the project managers, when the car doors opened, Mughniyeh was not alone: Iranian commander Soleimani and the Syrian nuclear coordinator Suleiman exited the vehicle with him. At the command center in Tel Aviv, the order was given: Hold.

The three buddies went up to the apartment. In Tel Aviv, the Mossad project managers and their CIA liaison waited, nervously biting their nails, on the verge of losing hope. A few hours later, the information arrived that Soleimani and Suleiman had left the apartment and been picked up by a car. The planners could now only pray that Mughniyeh would not remain in the apartment overnight.

About half an hour later, the surveillance team reported that Mughniyeh had entered the parking lot and approached his car.
In Tel Aviv, the order rang out: "Pe'al!"

The master terrorist, the Hezbollah commander whose trademark was car bombing, fell victim to his own craft in a blast of poetic justice.

Kill Olmert

Mughniyeh's successor, Mustafa Badr Adin, ordered attacks on Israeli embassies and tried to assassinate Olmert and senior Israeli military officers and officials.

But Badr Adin repeatedly failed. His only success was in 2012 at Burgas airport in Bulgaria, when a Hezbollah suicide bomber killed five Israeli tourists and their Bulgarian driver.

Security precautions around Olmert were stepped up last year out of concern that Hezbollah would attempt to get at him. Olmert was in office not only at the time of the Mughniyeh killing but during the month-long war between Israel and Hezbollah in 2006.

Olmert, who is now facing additional corruption charges after being indicted in an Israeli court, is loathed by the majority of Israelis. But analysts who watch the country's security and defense policies believe that in those areas he was far-sighted, showed determination, and was willing to take risks.

In September 2007, just five months before ordering the assassination of Mughniyeh, Olmert unleashed Israel's covert operatives and then the air force to destroy the Syrian nuclear reactor that North Korea had helped build in a remote area.

One can only imagine what the world would look like had the reactor been built and operated in an area now controlled by the brutal Islamic State.

Six months after Mughniyeh's assassination, Olmert approved a covert operation in which Israeli long-range snipers – apparently firing from a ship – assassinated Syria's nuclear coordinator, Gen. Suleiman, while he dined with guests on the balcony of his villa overlooking the Mediterranean.

Days after Mughniyeh was killed, then Vice President Dick Cheney called Olmert and they exchanged congratulations for the successful operation. President Bush, too, held Olmert in high respect – reportedly telling someone he liked the Israeli leaders because "he has balls."

The man of Mossad

The alleged Israeli spy who reportedly infiltrated Hezbollah and frustrated attacks against Israel held a number of important positions, including supervising the personal security of the organization's leader, Hassan Nasrallah.

The alleged Mossad member was reportedly arrested weeks ago and held the position of deputy chief of Unit 910, which carries out operations against specific Israeli targets.

Mohammed Shawraba was a resident of a village in south Lebanon and comes from a family that includes religious figures known for their loyalty to Hezbollah. But sources added that Mohammed Shawraba arrest would not hurt his family, which "cannot be blamed for his deeds."

He reportedly advanced in Hezbollah until he became responsible for Nasrallah's personal security with an emphasis on surveillance.

After the spy was discovered, Hezbollah was quick to discharge the unit's fighters and spread them around to other units. The commander was similarly discharged after the spy reported his activities to US and Israeli intelligence.

The espionage involved more than one person – a cell – that was "the most serious [intelligence] breach in Hezbollah's history." Under questioning, it was revealed that Mossad made periodic payments totaling $1 million. Mossad spy worked undercover as a businessman and traveled a great deal.

Mossad allegedly recruited Mohammed Shawraba in a western Asian country. He worked with Mossad for a number of years and foiled many Hezbollah operations that were meant to avenge the assassination of commander Imad Mughniyeh in Damascus in 2008.

The double agent also supposedly exposed information about operatives operating abroad, leading to the arrest of Hezbollah agent Muhammad Amadar in Lima, Peru, in October.

The recurring failures of Unit 910 "caused a state of frustration in the party's ranks," and led to the creation of a separate secret unit run by Iran's Revolutionary Guards.

After close monitoring of the most important security officials, the unit arrested five Hezbollah members including the [Unit 910 deputy chief]. Hezbollah refuses to deny or confirm reports that Shawraba fed the Mossad intelligence on the Lebanese group's foreign-operations unit, which he had headed since 2008.

He was arrested with four people who worked for him in the group's foreign-operations unit, which works against Israeli interests in foreign countries, the newspaper reported. It said Hezbollah had become suspicious of Shawraba after five attempted retaliations against Israel over the Mughniyeh killing had failed.

Counter Espionage

On Jan. 5 2015, Hezbollah's deputy chief Naim Qassem lauded the ability of a group as "big and sophisticated" as Hezbollah "to stand with the same steadfastness despite some major infiltrations." Media outlets identified the latest accused spy as Mohammad Shorbah, but as Qassem implied, this was not the first such "major infiltration," nor is it likely to be the last.

But Israel doesn't always come out on top in this intelligence war. Hezbollah is no slouch when it comes to espionage and counter-intelligence, the result of training its operatives receive from Iran's Ministry of Intelligence and Security, and Hezbollah has enjoyed its share of successes against Israeli and Western security agencies.

In late 2000, a retired Israeli colonel named Elhanan Tannenbaum established a shady business relationship with Qais Obeid, a Palestinian criminal with ties to Hezbollah. Tannenbaum was lured first to Brussels, then the United Arab Emirates, where he was kidnapped and smuggled to Lebanon.

"I inform you gladly," Hezbollah leader Hassan Nasrallah announced at a Beirut conference, that Hezbollah now held an Israeli Army officer with ties to Israeli security agencies who was captured "in a new qualitative achievement and in a complicated security operation." Tannenbaum's kidnapping was an intelligence bonanza for Hezbollah. After three years, Tannenbaum and the bodies of the three soldiers were exchanged for 435 prisoners in Israeli jails.

In fact, Hezbollah's intelligence prowess dates back much earlier, and has targeted not only Israeli but also American intelligence services. In the mid-

1990s, U.S. authorities investigating a local Hezbollah cell in New York quietly flew to South America on a lead. As soon as they landed they were paged by the New York field office. Photographs of the agents disembarking had just arrived on the office's fax machine in New York. More recently, in June of 2011, Nasrallah claimed that Hezbollah had identified at least two CIA spies within the group's ranks. "No one underestimates [Hezbollah's] capabilities," said one U.S. official at the time.

Nevertheless, the litany of failed Hezbollah operations over the past few years suggests Hezbollah's covert operational prowess has diminished. Public slip-ups included plots in Azerbaijan, India, Thailand and Egypt. Hezbollah agents were picked up by local authorities in Azerbaijan, Cyprus, Nigeria and Thailand and are now convicted felons serving jail time. More Hezbollah plots were thwarted this past year in Thailand and Peru — to cite just some of the recently foiled Hezbollah operations. Hezbollah's only success was the 2012 bombing of a tour bus in Burgas, Bulgaria.

Mughniyeh Sr. was killed in 2008, and Mughniyeh Jr. in 2015; Shorbah was arrested in 2014. Individual battles are won and lost, but the spy-vs-spy intelligence war between Hezbollah and Israel continues. Both sides see themselves as battling for survival, which means the espionage war is likely to continue at full force. In the words of espionage novelist John Le Carre, "Survival … is an infinite capacity for suspicion" — and there's no shortage of suspicion between Israel and Hezbollah.

Jihad Mughniyeh

In January 18, 2014 six officers killed by two missiles fired by Israeli helicopters over the Golan near Quneitra: Mohammed Issa, a Hizballah commander responsible for its Syrian and Iraqi operations, Jihad Mughniyeh, the son of Imad Mughniyeh, a top Hizbullah operative killed in a 2008 car bombing in Syria blamed on Israel; Mahdi al-Moussawi, Ali Fouad, Hussein Hassan and Abbas Hijazi. Iranian commander Abu Ali al-Tabtabani was among the dead.

An Israeli security source said that a helicopter had carried out a strike against terrorists in the Syrian sector of the Golan who were preparing an attack on Israel. The missile strike hit a Hezbollah convoy in the Syrian province of Quneitra, near the Israeli-occupied Golan Heights.

Quneitra has seen heavy fighting between forces loyal to Assad and rebels including fighters linked to al Qaeda. Israel has struck Syria several times since the start of the war, mostly destroying weaponry such as missiles that Israeli officials said were destined for Hezbollah, Israel's long-time foe in neighbouring Lebanon. Syria said that Israeli jets had bombed areas near Damascus international airport and in the town of Dimas, near the border with Lebanon.

Three months after being killed in an attack attributed to Israel, new details emerge about Hezbollah's Golan region commander, who was working with Iran's Revolutionary Guard on high-profile attacks against IDF. Among the attacks were four successful rocket launches at Israel and a number of successful mortar attacks on Israel; all of which fell in open areas during Operation Protective Edge in the summer.

Israel knew Mughniyeh was traveling in the jeep convey together with a top Iranian general and Abu Issa, the man who coordinates Hezbollah activities in the Golan. The Syrian general who was also traveling with them was said to be in charge of training the forces which was said they were planning attacks inside Israeli territory as well as additional rocket fire.

The day of the alleged Israeli attack, the group had conducted an observation patrol of Israel as part of their attempts to plan attacks against Israel. Until the Mughniyeh-led taskforce, Iran had attempted to use local proxies to wage war on Israel, mostly through pro-Palestinian forces, most famously Samir Kuntar, vis-à-vis their support of Hezbollah.

These small cells managed to carry out a number of attacks against Israel in the past year and a half, mostly by laying blasts along the border and detonating them in proximity to IDF forces. However, over time these attacks dwindled down, as Israel began exacting revenge against the Syrian army, which were usually hit by the IDF in response.

Hezbollah's presence along Israel's northern border from Syria, in addition to their homeland of Lebanon, is viewed by Israel as an ongoing potential threat. Despite Jerusalem's policy of neutrality in regards to the Syrian conflict, on a number of occasions foreign reports have said Israel targeted Hezbollah conveys or arms warehouses, which some have claimed contained "game-changing" weapons.

Among the Hezbollah, Jihad Mughniyeh was known as "the prince" and his military career (still at the beginning) was personally followed by the leader of the organization, Hassan Nasrallah, who was a sort of godfather figure.

Recently, he had been entrusted with the command of a brigade in Syria's Golan right in front of the Israeli lines. According to Hezbollah's media outlet al-Manar, his unit was hit by Israeli rockets as it was patrolling the village of Mazrat al-Amal, near Kuneitra, the Syrian capital of Golan - just a few kilometers from Israeli postings on the occupied heights. In Israel, few details have been released on the incident.

Military radio only confirmed that the Israeli air force carried out an attack and State television added that the raid thus "foiled an attack". Many have said that members of Iran's Revolutionary Guard Corps were on the ground.

The unit could be have been searching the area to find locations to place land-attack missiles able to reach a target inside Israel. Such missiles have been reportedly deployed in southern Lebanon for years but Hezbollah would now like to extend its offensive capacity in the Syrian Golan. "The Lebanese and Syrian front are one thing for us at this point", a military source told Israeli State television.

Hezbollah fighters in towns and villages along the border with Israel went on high alert following the strike, said an official from the group. In the Shi'ite-dominated areas of south Lebanon and Beirut, the streets emptied quickly as residents feared an escalation. Hezbollah-run Al-Manar TV warned that Israel was "playing with fire that puts the security of the whole Middle East on edge."

The strike came three days after Hezbollah leader Hassan Nasrallah said he considered frequent Israeli strikes in Syria as major acts of aggression, and that Syria and its allies had the right to respond. Hezbollah has been fighting alongside President Bashar Assad's forces in Syria's nearly four-year-old civil war. Israel has struck Syria several times since the start of the conflict, mostly destroying weaponry such as missiles that Israeli officials said were destined for their long-time foe Hezbollah in neighboring Lebanon.

The air strike targeted two Hezbollah vehicles as fighters were inspecting positions in the Golan Heights, close to the Israeli-controlled frontier. A Syrian activist said Hezbollah was widely rumored to be training pro-Assad militiamen and Syrian government forces near the area.

Last October, it was reported that Jihad Mughniyeh was appointed to head Hezbollah's Golan division. The reports emerged from Syrian opposition groups and were not confirmed by Hezbollah. Mohad Razlan, a senior official in the Syrian National Council, said at the time that the appointment stemmed from Hezbollah's decision to expand its operations.

Maj. Gen. (res.) Yoav Galant, a former head of IDF Southern Command, hinted in an interview with Channel 2 that the timing of the strike was linked to the upcoming Knesset election. "Based on past incidents, one can deduce that sometimes the timing isn't entirely unconnected to the election," he said.

Galant, who is running for Knesset as part of the Kulanu party, further insinuated that the IDF's assassination of Hamas commander Ahmed Jabari in November 2012 was timed to take place just before an election. Galant said there had been numerous opportunities to carry out the operation long before the election campaign.

Economy Minister Naftali Bennett dismissed Galant's statements as politically motivated. He called on Kulanu party leader Moshe Kahlon to order Galant to retract them "before damage is caused." Bennett had no comment on the reports of the air strike. Defense Minister Moshe Ya'alon, too, refused to address the incident directly.

"Every time something happens in the region, we are blamed," he told Kol Hai Radio. "I have no interest in addressing this. We have heard [Hezbollah leader] Hassan Nasrallah's speech last week. He denied the presence of Hezbollah operatives in the Golan. If this is true, he has some explaining to do."

In December 2014, Syrian media reported that an Israeli drone had been brought down in Quneitra province. The report showed footage of what looked like an Israeli Skylark 1 model unmanned aerial vehicle. The IDF said at the time it had no knowledge of a UAV that was downed in Syria.

According to Syrian media, the Israel Air Force flew at least 10 sorties over the Dimas area and attacked several military targets. Residents of Damascus reported hearing loud explosions on the outskirts of the city.

Israel Desk

The Director of the Israel Desk of the Revolutionary Guards clandestine service was executed by a firing squad in late June or early July 2015 after he was accused of spying for Israel.

Aged 46, Seyyed Ahmed Dabiri was his codename. His real name is not known. The sources report that he was tried by a Guards martial court and found guilty of tipping Israel off on classified information, including the movements of Iranian military commanders in Syria, Iranian arms shipments to Syria and arms convoys bound for Hizballah in Lebanon.

Suspicion first fell on Dabiri after the Israeli air force struck the convoy of Iranian and Hizballah commanders that was on a top-secret visit to the village of Mazraat Amal near the Golan town of Quneitra on Jan. 18. They were there to survey the terrain preparatory to planting a Hizballah rocket position just across from IDF's Golan outposts, a mission which ended in disaster.

After the air strike, the plan was abandoned, a setback with devastating effect on the Iranian and Hizballah high commands. Hizballah chief Hassan Nasrallah announced at the time that the gloves was now off against Israel and that "rules of engagement" with the Jewish state were no longer in force.

No more than a handful of big shots were privy to the Golan tour in the highest Revolutionary Guards highest echelon and the inner circle of Nasrallah. The IRGC's chief Gen. Ali Jafari and Iran's Middle East commander in chief Gen.

Qassem Suleimani ordered an all-encompassing investigation to find out who was responsible for leaking to Israeli intelligence the secret of the Golan tour. The high Hizballah command and the Guards headquarters in Tehran were exhaustively investigated.

A short time earlier, in December 2014, Mohammad Shawraba, 42, the deputy chief of Unit 910, which is responsible for external terrorist operations, was arrested on suspicion of spying for Israel.

So in the weeks leading up to the Israeli Golan attack, Hizballah was buzzing with Israeli spy fever. Yet the Guards probe failed to discover the source of the leak either in Beirut or Tehran. When no Israeli mole was identified, the Guards intelligence chief Gen. Hassan Taeb set a trap and baited it with a false piece of intelligence.

On April 25, Israel air planes struck what they believed to be Syrian and Hizballah bases and arms dumps in the Qalamoun Mountains on the Syrian-Lebanese border. Middle East media carried confused reports on this attack – some claiming it targeted an arms convoy heading into Lebanon from Syria; others cited missile stores or even the Syrian army's 155th and 65th Brigades. Israeli sources declined to confirm or deny any of those versions.

The cause of the mix-up was that the target was a red herring. But the attack enabled Iranian spy catchers to narrow down the source and discover that Ahmad Dabiri was the mole who had tipped Israel off.

Mohammed Ali Allahdadi

Mohammed Ali Allahdadi, a senior Iranian general serving as an adviser to the Syrian army, died along with five other Iranians and six Hezbollah officers in the January 18, 2015 strike on Quneitra.

According to the Lebanese newspaper Al Joumhouria, an investigation conducted by the Shi'ite group Hezbollah concluded that Allahdadi had kept his phone on, despite him being in an area monitored intensively by Israeli intelligence, meaning that it was possible to determining his whereabouts. The Israeli army has neither confirmed nor denied the reports that it was responsible for the strike.

Allahdadi was on the Syrian side of the Golan Heights with Hezbollah members visiting outposts constructed as a measure against rebels fighting the Assad regime. According to the Maariv report, another Iranian officer – in charge of transcribing the protocols agreed between the officials present during the tour, in particular Allahdadi's instructions – was also killed in the strike.

The death of Brigadier General Mohammad-Ali Allah-Dadi, the latest Islamic Revolutionary Guard Corps Qods Force (IRGC-QF) officer killed abroad, has generated an outpouring of condolences and support from Iran's political and military elite.

Allah-Dadi, who had a distinguished career and solid Iran-Iraq War background, was killed by an Israeli helicopter assault in the Syrian city of Quneitra, in the Golan Heights. Senior Iranian officials have and are continuing to weigh in on the event, brandishing Iranian deterrence and even threatening retaliation against Israel in their statements.

The Secretary of Iran's Supreme National Security Council (SNSC), Admiral Ali Shamkhani, claimed that "the current of resistance would answer the terrorist action of the Zionist regime with revolutionary intensity and determination in a time and place of our choosing." Such open-ended threats were not limited to Shamkhani. In a prepared statement, Major General Mohammad-Ali Aziz-Jafari, the Commander of Iran's IRGC proclaimed that "These martyrdoms have proved that we must not distance ourselves from Jihad; the Zionists must await our destructive thunderbolts, in the past they have seen the emergence of our anger."

Brigadier General Esmail Qaani, the Deputy Qods Force Commander echoed Shamkhani's sentiments, adding a twist of his own against Israel: "We will certainly provide the answer to your brashness and thuggery in our own time and place, and know that we will be [the] file against your spirit and life."

Even former President Ali-Akbar Hashemi Rafsanjani, the current Chairman of the Expediency Discernment Council, used similar language, as he proclaimed, "To quote the Secretary-General of Lebanon's Hezbollah, the Zionists [should] go prepare their refuge."

Framing the strike as part of an attempt to blunt Iran's regional preeminence was Brigadier General Hossein Salami, the IRGC Deputy Commander who stated, "The Zionists engaged in such a crime due to the defeats they have suffered from Hezbollah in Yemen, Bahrain, Iraq, and Syria." Salami too issued a warning: "The Zionists should know that they will see the ruinous thunderbolts of the IRGC in action, as in the past."

Praising Allah-Dadi more specifically, and linking his legacy to Iran's Islamic Revolution was Major General Mostafa Izadi, a Deputy in Iran's General Staff Armed Forces, who eulogized that "The martyr [Shahid] Allah-Dadi was the type of person who really knew himself, and found this luck to be present in different stages of the Revolution."

An inspection of Allah-Dadi's recent arrival in the Syrian theater points to his having been tapped for the role by Qods Force Commander Major General Qassem Soleimani. Such affinity between Soleimani and Allah-Dadi helps to indicate why Soleimani took time out of his day as Qods Force Commander to personally perform the Ziarat-e Ashura prayer during Allah-Dadi's funeral service.

Additionally weighing-in was Hojjat al-Eslam Mohammad-Hassan Abutorabi Fard, the Deputy-Speaker of Iran's Parliament. Implying that Hezbollah would be in charge of the response, he noted: "Until present, the Zionists have received several slaps from the Islamic Resistance and Hezbollah, and the response of Hezbollah to this Zionist crime will be exceptional and special."

Parliamentary Speaker Ali Larijani on the other hand, chose to praise Allah-Dadi's "martyrdom" without linking it to a threat against Israel. The same went for Yazd Governor Seyyed Mohammad Mir Mohammadi, in charge of the city housing the Al-Ghadir IRGC unit which Allah-Dadi formerly commanded. Mir Mohammadi stated: "Martyrdom is the art of men of God."

Iranian cabinet ministers too, have offered their condolences. Foreign Minister Mohammad-Javad Zarif called the attack an "insane act," while Intelligence Minister Hojjat al-Eslam Alavi stated that Allah-Dadi was killed while engaged in "an advisory function to help the innocent government and nation of Syria against Takfiri-Salafi terrorists."

And of course, the set of condolences included those of Hossein Dehqan, Iran's Minister of Defense. Dehqan's history of support to Hezbollah is well-known, as evidenced by his recent reference to Israeli activity in Quneitra circa 1982. Dehqan stated that "This terrorist action of the Zionist regime in the Golan [Heights] is the continuation of the crimes of the regime in Palestine, Syria, Iraq, [and] Lebanon."

Recently, pictures have emerged from the ceremonies and funeral service of Mohammad-Ali Allah-Dadi. One notable photo is of current and former IRGC Commanders (skipping over Yahya-Rahim Safavi) Rezaie and Jafari. At the service, Major General Jafari took his praise of Allahdadi in a different direction than his earlier prepared commentary. While it is expected for the Islamic Republic's elite to praise their deceased colleague and continue their vitriol against Israel, Jafari morphed Allah-Dadi's death abroad into part of the foreign policy legacy of the Islamic Republic: "The Islamic Revolution outside the country's borders is advancing with speed and is after the conquest of fortifications, and is the realization of the ideals of the deceased Imam (Ayatollah Khomeini) and the martyrs."

Samir Kuntar

Top Hezbollah operative, Samir Kuntar, 53, who was responsible for one of the most traumatic terror attacks in Israeli history, has been killed in a Syrian airstrike on Damascus on Saturday December 19, 2015, which Hezbollah sources are claiming was carried out by the Israeli Defense Forces.

Israeli officials praised the assassination, though were unable to confirm whether Israel was responsible for the attack. Energy Minister Yuval Steinitz said he would not be sorry if the reports of Israel's involvement turned out to be true. "Kuntar was an evil man," he said before a cabinet meeting. "It's possible that Finnish intelligence was at work here, and did a good job."

Israelis' abhorrence of Kuntar spans back nearly three decades, when he led and orchestrated one of the most ruthless attacks that still lives in the Israeli consciousness. In the cover of darkness on April 22, 1979, Kuntar, then 16, led a Palestinian Liberation Front attack that brutally murdered a family in the northern town of Nahariya and an Israeli police officer. From southern Lebanon, Kuntar and his accomplices snuck into Israel via the sea, and then broke into a family's apartment. There, they kidnapped a young father, Danny Haran, and his 4-year-old daughter Einat.

Kuntar took the father and his young daughter to the nearby beach. There, he shot the father, and had the daughter, Einat, watch as he drowned her father underwater to ensure he was completely dead. Then, he smashed the young girl's head against a nearby rock with the butt of his gun.

As Kuntar was kidnapping the father and daughter, the mother, Samadar, grabbed their 2-year old baby, Yael, and hid from the men who breached her home. As Samadar tried to keep her baby quiet to keep them from being found, her daughter suffocated in her arms. Kuntar was caught after a shootout with police, but the damage was done. By morning, one out of the four Harans was left alive.

Israelis still identify this attack as one of the most brutal in the history of the Jewish state. But that is not the end of Kuntar's tale. In 1985, four members of the PLF hijacked the Achille Lauro cruise ship sailing from Alexandria, Egypt to Ashdod, in southern Israel, in an attempt to gain negotiating power for Kuntar's release. The attempt was unsuccessful, but the assailants killed a disabled, wheelchair- bound American Jewish passenger, Leon Klinghoffer. A hotly contested opera of the hijacking and the murder, "The Death of Klinghoffer," was performed at the Metropolitan Opera in New York City last season, much to the chagrin of right wing activists groups, claiming the libretto was anti-Semitic. In this, the hijacking's legacy lives on.

Two decades later, after several failed negotiation attempts, Kuntar was freed. In 2008, Kuntar along with four other Hezbollah operatives was released in a prisoner exchange to return the bodies of Israeli soldiers Eldad Regev and Ehud Goldwasser, who were abducted by Hezbollah in a cross-border operation that sparked the Second Lebanon War.

Upon Kuntar's release, he received a hero's welcome in Lebanon and Syria, being personally received by Lebanese President Michel Suleiman and by Hezbollah leader Hasan Nasrallah, and receiving Syria's highest medal from President Bashar Assad. In 2009, he was awarded an honorary salute by former Iranian President Mahmoud Ahmadinejad during a ceremony in honor of former political prisoners.

Soon thereafter, Kuntar joined and started climbing the ranks in Hezbollah, and repeatedly pledged to 'confront' Israel. For years, he was quoted as calling Israel a "disease" that needs to be taken care of. Kuntar, Arab media reports, has quietly been responsible for building infrastructure near the Golan Heights in order to launch attacks against Israel, and has been fighting on behalf of the Assad regime in the current Syrian civil war.

Strong Iran

Kuntar, who was convicted of murdering four Israelis in a 1979 terror attack and was released by Israel as part of a prisoner exchange deal in 2008, was referring to comments by the Iranian Supreme Leader, when he called Israel a "cancerous tumor" that should be removed.

Netanyahu said Khamenei's remarks "strengthen the steadfastness of my government on the security needs of Israel's citizens and our demand that Israel be recognized as a Jewish state."

Speaking on the sidelines of the Tehran conference on the Palestinian Intifada, Kuntar remarked on the swiftness of Netanyahu's response, tells the semi-official Fars Iranian news agency that "Ayatollah Khamenei's statements horrified the Zionist regime, otherwise we would not witness Netanyahu's rapid reaction."

He also stressed Iran's importance in the effort to free Palestinian land from Israeli occupation, saying that the "existence of a powerful Iran will no doubt help to the settlement of the Palestinian issue and the victory of resistance."

Kuntar's remarks came a day after Iranian President Mahmoud Ahmadinejad was quoted by AFP as saying that if "the backers of the Zionist regime want to solve the issue... the solution is simple ... everyone should go home. Some poor people were brought to Palestine on the promise of security and jobs while they made Palestinian people into refugees... So now Palestinians should go home and those brought here should go to theirs," Ahmadinejad was quoted by AFP.

Ahmadinejad was also quoted by the IRNA news agency as questioning whether or not the Palestinian-Israeli conflict was in fact had to involve Western countries.

"Is the Palestinian issue and Arab issue or a problem between the Arab nations on the one side and some western countries on the other side?" the Iranian president asked, "or it is a problem between Arab nations on the one hand and some Jews who have occupied the Palestinian lands on the other."

Target "Samir"

Syrian and Hizballah media confirmed that Israeli rocket fire from four air force jets early Sunday, Dec. 20, destroyed a building in the eastern Jaramana district of Damascus and killed Samir Kuntar, head of Hizballah networks in southern Syria and the Golan. Footage showed a multi-storey residential building collapsed and rescue workers digging through the rubble for survivors. In addition to Kuntar, Issam Sha'alan, a senior commander of the National Syrian Golan Resistance Organization was also killed. This organization was established by Syrian intelligence for operations against Israel.

In the last two years, Samir Quntar established a network of cells in all of southern Syria on behalf of three masters: Iran's Revolutionary Guards, Hizballah and the Assad regime's Military Intelligence Agency.

In Tehran and Damascus, his mission was defined as "establishing commando units for special operations." Those units were in fact hit-cum-terror squads. His territory ranged from Jebel Druze in southeast Syria up to the Druze villages of the Syrian Hermon range and the Syrian Golan including Quneitra. In the past year, he recruited scores of Syrian Druze to fight for Bashar Assad and was able to prevent the Druze community from joining the rebel forces fighting the Assad regime in southern Syria. He was outstandingly successful in thwarting every US-Jordanian-Israeli action for deploying an effective military force to the rear of the Syrian army in the South.

The renegade Druze terrorist additionally mustered Druze recruits to his terror cells in 30 villages on the Hermon opposite IDF positions. These cells were responsible for the intermittent short-range rocket fire into the Israeli Golan and Galilee. They caused slight damage but they were an effective stratagem in his drive to plant his spies in the Druze villages and turn them against relations with the IDF and Syrian rebel forces.

Kuntar acted under the direct command of the Al Qods Brigades chief the Iranian general Qassem Soleimani, after he was appointed commander of Iranian forces in Syria, Lebanon and Iraq, and Mustafa Badr, Al-Din, head of Hizballah forces in Syria.

He was recently promoted to take charge of building a combined terrorist network of Syrians, Hizballah commandos and Palestinians for mounting incursions deep into Israel for major terrorist attacks. His transfer from southern Syria to a high security residential building in Damascus attested to his enhanced status.

Reactions

Hizballah chief Hassan Nasrallah said: "We clearly and openly accuse the Zionist enemy of assassinating Samir al-Kuntar... We have no doubt that the Israeli enemy was behind the assassination in a blatant military operation." He went on to say: "It is our right to retaliate to Quntar's assassination at the appropriate time and place and in the appropriate way and we will practice this right," he said, alleging that the master terrorist was killed by a guided missile fired from Israeli warplanes.

Nasrallah's unscheduled speech followed the mass funeral of the late commander of Hizballah's terrorist networks in southern Syria and the Golan Damascus Sunday night.

Hassan Nasrallah said: "Revenge for the death of Samir Quntar is on the way… The orders have been given and execution is in the hands of resistance fighters on the ground… We are not afraid of consequences and threats. We shall not let the blood of our Jihadi fighters and brothers to be spilled anywhere in the world." Nasrallah went on to say: "The Israelis are worried and rightly so - those on the borders [soldiers] and those inside the country… They decided that eliminating such an important target is worth the adventure and the sacrifice…They thought that al-Kuntar is not that important to Hizballah."

The Hizballah leader maintained that Prime Minister Binyamin Netanyahu thought he could take advantage of the Syrian war to win international recognition for Israel's annexation of the Golan. "As we commemorate al-Kuntar, we must revive the spirit of sacrifice because that is a key condition of the rise of the people, the persistence of resistance and the creation of the future." Nasrallah called on the Palestinians to stop waiting for pro-Western Arab nations to take action, or for American operations in concert with Arab regimes

On Alert

The IDF and all of the armies involved in the Syrian civil war, namely those of Russia, Syria and Iran, went on their highest war alert on Thursday, Dec. 31 when all their intelligence organizations reported that Hassan Nasrallah could not be stopped from attacking Israel, in revenge for the assassination of Samir Kuntar in Damascus on December 20.

More than one intermediary visited Beirut to avert the Hizballah attack and its deadly fallout, including a former senior officer of the German BND foreign intelligence service. Gerhard Conrad, late of the BND and incumbent director of the European Union's Intelligence and Situation Center, was given this urgent mission by Chancellor Angela Merkel.

He came away from a meeting with Nasrallah on Dec. 29, with the news that the Hizballah chief was not open to persuasion and the attack was already underway.

Conrad has excellent connections in the Arab world, especially in Syria and Lebanon. Seven years ago, he acted as intermediary between Israel and Hizballah for negotiating the recovery of the bodies of two fallen IDF soldiers, Eldad Regev and Ehud Goldwasser, in exchange for the handover of that same Hizballah high-up Samir Quntar and other jailed and convicted Arab terrorists.

The German spy-diplomat then established personal connections with a shadowy figure, Wafik Safa, who is in charge of Hizballah's intelligence and security network and a close crony of Nasrallah.

Conrad used those connections again in 2011 to broker the release of Gilead Shalit from Hamas captivity. It was Safa he arranged for him to meet Nasrallah in Beirut. He found the Hizballah chief unshakeable in his determination to make Israel pay for Kuntar's death, even at the cost of a painful backlash against the Shiite group's terrorists in Syria and Lebanon.

He was unmoved by the warning issued by Israel's chief of staff, Lieut. Gen. Gady Eisenkott, on Monday, just hours before the Conrad mission. Eisenkott said, "Just as we have proven in the past, we know how to strike anyone who wishes to harm us. Our enemies know they will suffer grave consequences if they try to undermine our security."

Upon receipt of the German emissary's report on the meeting, Eisenkott, his deputy, Maj. Gen. Yair Golan, and OC Northern Command, Maj. Gen. Aviv Kochavi, inspected the preparedness of the IDF's northern border defenses for all contingencies.

Russian military and Iranian Revolutionary Guard forces in Syria have taken into account that a Hizballah attack will not go unanswered by Israel and that the IDF would most likely hit back at Hizballah on Syrian soil, thus ushering in the New Year with a new whirlwind.

The Hizballah leader Hassan Nasrallah's eulogy for Samir Quntar at his funeral Monday, Dec. 21 was not only brief but also untraditional. After blaming Israel in a few short sentences for assassinating him, Nasrallah said he would laud the Kuntar's deeds and qualities on another occasion. That was hardly the tribute the Hizballah would normally have awarded a senior operative killed by Zionist missiles.

Kuntar had of late transferred his services from Hizballah to the Iranian Revolutionary Guards. He kept up his connections in Hizballah, but took orders from the Iranians in preference to instructions from Nasrallah and the commander of Hizballah operations in Syria, Mustafa Badr al-Din.

The Iranian command in Damascus provided him with two apartments in the Jamaran district south of the Syrian capital, where he lived and worked. But he was also given two Iranian handlers, officers of Gen. Qassem Soleimani's Al Qods Brigades.

The two Iranian officers, Mohammed Riza Fahemi and Mir Ahmad Ahmadi, died in the rocket attack Sunday, Dec. 20, along with Quntar and his deputy, Farhan Issam Sha'alan, head of the "Syrian National Resistance on the Golan" organization, which was just then getting ready to launch attacks deep inside Israeli territory.

Wednesday, Dec. 23, the IDF raised the level of alert another notch on the Golan, the Lebanese and Syrian borders and on the main roads of northern Israel, in view of signs that the Iranian leadership was bent on avenging the loss of Kuntar and the two Iranian intelligence officers.

High Iranian officials had concluded that Israel had targeted Kuntar to get at Tehran, rather than Hizballah. It was seen as a warning from Jerusalem that if the new terrorist network that Kuntar had established, in partnership with Syria and Hizballah, went into action against Israel, Iran would pay a price: more elements of its military and intelligence structure in Syria would be targeted. Iran's leaders also decided, according to those sources, that the deaths of Kuntar and two Iranian officers must not go unpunished.

But the rushed eulogy and unceremonious funeral also had a hidden context. Although the dead man was a member of the Druze faith, the ceremony was conducted according to Shiite rites at Hizballah's main center of worship, the Shite Hosniyeh mosque in southern Beirut. The hundreds of thousands of Syrian, Lebanese and Israeli Druze who witnessed the ceremony were appalled to discover that Kuntar had deserted his ancestral faith and converted to Shiite Muslim.

Kuntar kept his conversion a deep secret, known to no one in the Druze community, only to a handful of top Iranian and Hizballah officials. Since the secret has come out, his compatriots in Syria, Lebanon and the Golan feel they were cheated by Iranian and Hizballah agents into following Kuntar, in the false belief that he headed an autonomous Druze group, when in fact he was a renegade and the minion of a Shiite power.

What next?

Israeli communities on the northern border were on high alert following the killing of Lebanese Druze Samir Kuntar. The defense establishment braced for Hezbollah's reaction, and sure enough, three rockets were fired at the northern city of Nahariya on Sunday afternoon. But everyone knows this sporadic fire was just an appetizer, and that the real retaliation has yet to come.

Based on reports in Lebanese media, Kuntar's elimination was an impressive operation on all levels: the preliminary intelligence gathering, the real-time pinpointing of his location, and the surgical strike, which entailed minimal collateral damage. Two of his partners in his efforts to establish a Druze-based terrorist infrastructure in the Golan Heights (his spokesman and a guard) were also killed in the strike.

For over a year, Kuntar has been laying the foundations for a terrorist network designed to target Israel, and in 2014 his operatives carried out nine attacks against Israel -- five involving roadside bombs and four of rocket fire. While most of the earlier infrastructure had been eliminated by Israel, the defense establishment was monitoring ongoing attempts to establish the so-called "national Syrian resistance in the Golan" closely.

If the foreign media reports attributing Kuntar's demise to Israel are true, than it was most likely not an operation of revenge for his past crimes, so much as a pre-emptive strategy to thwart the terrorist attacks he had in the works.

Once back in Lebanon, Hezbollah tasked Kuntar with developing its infrastructure in Judea and Samaria, but those efforts proved futile, and Kuntar was given a new mission, more in line with Hezbollah's overall operations -- doing Iran's bidding.

Whatever response the Shiite terrorist group will mount over the killing of Kuntar will, to a great extent, reflect Tehran's interests. Nevertheless, Iran finds itself in a situation where its interests are crossed, as it must also consider the implications retaliation might have on the nuclear deal with the West, and more importantly, on its primary regional interest -- preserving the regime of Syrian President Bashar Assad.

The fact that Hezbollah will most likely be left to its own devices on this matter should be very disconcerting for Israel. While Hezbollah did not hold Kuntar in the same regard as Jihad Mughniyeh (whose killing in January triggered Hezbollah to respond with the killing of two Israeli soldiers), the group has set a certain retaliatory bar for itself, one it cannot afford to fall under.

Past experience has shown that eventually Hezbollah will find a target, in which case Israel will be left to decide its next move. In January, it was decided to contain the situation and avoid an escalation on the northern border. This decision was based on the assumption that Hezbollah would also prefer to avoid a flare-up in the area. This dilemma may present itself again, perhaps sooner than Israel wanted.